THE IVY LEAGUE

THE IVY LEAGUE

AN EXPOSITION OF PSALM 91,
Volume 4

IDOWU ILUYOMADE

XULON PRESS

Xulon Press
2301 Lucien Way #415
Maitland, FL 32751
407.339.4217
www.xulonpress.com

© 2020 by Idowu Iluyomade

All rights reserved solely by the author. The author guarantees all contents are original and do not infringe upon the legal rights of any other person or work. No part of this book may be reproduced in any form without the permission of the author. The views expressed in this book are not necessarily those of the publisher.

Unless otherwise indicated, Scripture quotations taken from the King James Version (KJV) – *public domain*.

Scripture quotations taken from The Message (MSG). Copyright © 1993, 1994, 1995, 1996, 2000, 2001, 2002. Used by permission of NavPress Publishing Group. Used by permission. All rights reserved.

Scripture quotations taken from the Holy Bible, New Living Translation (NLT). Copyright ©1996, 2004, 2007 by Tyndale House Foundation. Used by permission of Tyndale House Publishers, Inc.

Scripture quotations taken from the Amplified Bible (AMP). Copyright © 1954, 1958, 1962, 1964, 1965, 1987 by The Lockman Foundation. Used by permission. All rights reserved.

Scripture quotations taken from the Holy Bible, New International Version (NIV). Copyright © 1973, 1978, 1984, 2011 by Biblica, Inc.™. Used by permission. All rights reserved.

Printed in the United States of America.

ISBN-13: 978-1-6305-0753-4

Dedication

To God Almighty, on whose wings I will keep soaring higher; there is no stopping me.

TABLE OF CONTENTS

Dedication v
Acknowledgment xiii
Introduction..xv

Chapter 1:
The Eagle Flies Toward Heaven Above 1

Chapter 2:
The Anatomy of an Eagle 7

Chapter 3:
God's Nature in Man – Eagle is Fearless..................... 15

Chapter 4:
God's Nature in Man – Eagle is Strategic.................... 19

Chapter 5:
God's Nature in Man – Eagle Rides the Storm 29

Chapter 6:
God's Nature in Man – Eagle Stirreth up Her Nest............. 33

Chapter 7:
The Eagle Stirreth up Her Nest 37

Chapter 8:
The Re-birth of an Eagle 45

Books by the Author

Eat This (2010)
Expressions of Love (2010)
Not Ashamed (2016)
Caught Red Handed (2016)
The Audacity of Faith (2016)
Between the Mother Hen & Bad Mamas (2017)
At Last! (2017)
Pursue, Overtake & Recover All (2017)
God's Comprehensive Insurance Policy (2018)
Deliverance from the Snare of the Fowler (2018)
Christian Social Responsibility (2018)
Quest for the Truth (2019)
Finding True Love in a Love Recession (2019)
Bent but not Broken (2019)
Loving you Always (2019)

Psalm 91

He that dwelleth in the secret place of the Most High shall abide under the shadow of the Almighty.

I will say of the Lord, He is my refuge and my fortress: my God; in him will I trust.

Surely he shall deliver thee from the snare of the fowler, and from the noisome pestilence.

He shall cover thee with his feathers, and under his wings shalt thou trust: his truth shall be thy shield and buckler.

Thou shalt not be afraid for the terror by night; nor for the arrow that flieth by day;

Nor for the pestilence that walketh in darkness; nor for the destruction that wasteth at noonday.

A thousand shall fall at thy side, and ten thousand at thy right hand; but it shall not come nigh thee.

Only with thine eyes shalt thou behold and see the reward of the wicked.

Because thou hast made the Lord, which is my refuge, even the most High, thy habitation;

There shall no evil befall thee, neither shall any plague come nigh thy dwelling.

For He shall give His angels charge over thee, to keep thee in all thy ways.

They shall bear thee up in their hands, lest thou dash thy foot against a stone.

Thou shalt tread upon the lion and adder: the young lion and the dragon shalt thou trample under feet.

Because he hath set his love upon Me, therefore will I deliver him:

I will set him on high, because he hath known my name.

He shall call upon me, and I will answer him: I will be with him in trouble; I will deliver him, and honour him.

With long life will I satisfy him, and shew him My salvation.

Acknowledgments

I wish to first appreciate God, for giving me the inspiration to commence an in-depth, interactive study of the book of John. This was about twenty years ago. It's been my lifelong ambition to publish a workbook that would literally transpose readers into the unique setting and bustling atmosphere of our midweek services called "Digging for Gold." This is the platform we have been using for this unique style of teaching. We discovered that the Holy Spirit has so much to say to us, as prophesied by Jesus Christ. So much so that it has taken us almost ten years to cover just three chapters of the book of John.

I decided that, instead of waiting for the entire book to be published, we would present nuggets of the whole as modules. This is one of the modules that summarizes part of the various conversations that we had on the eagle.

I must acknowledge the contributions of our regular Tuesday congregants and the many online members who constitute our ever-growing virtual church. To you all, I say *thank you*.

To my sugar, I say *thank you* for all those pre-service private dissections of various topics for discussions.

To Jola, Todun, and Toju; our three wonderful children and most prized blessings from God.

To the team who put this book together, God bless you and reward your labour of love.

INTRODUCTION

According to Wikipedia, as of the 25th February 2019, the Ivy League is an American Collegiate Athletic Conference comprising sports teams from eight private universities in the northeastern United States. The term *Ivy League* is typically used to refer to eight schools as a group of elite colleges, beyond the sports context. The eight colleges are Brown University, Columbia University, Cornell University, Dartmouth College, Harvard University, the University of Pennsylvania, Princeton University, and Yale University. *Ivy League* has connotations of academic excellence, selectivity in admissions, and social elitism.

While the term was in use as early as 1933, it became official only after the formation of the NCAA Division I Athletic Conference in 1954. Seven of the eight schools were founded during the colonial period (Cornell was founded in 1865), and, thus, account for seven of the nine Colonial Colleges chartered before the American Revolution.

Ivy League schools are generally viewed as some of the most prestigious and are ranked among the best universities worldwide by U.S. News & World Report. All eight universities place in the top fourteen of the 2019 *U.S. News & World Report's* national university rankings, including four Ivy League institutions in the top three (Columbia and Yale are tied for third). The *Ivy League* is truly in a class of its own.

In this book, we will use an analogy of the eagle versus the hen.

Our studies of the book of John over the years took us to Psalm 91, which we believe contains the *Covenant of Peace* or *Comprehensive*

Insurance that God has with believers, on account of the death and resurrection of Jesus Christ. In Volume 3 of this series, titled, "Between the Mother Hen and the Bad Mamas," we analysed Psalm 91:4. Wherein, God is described in the likeness of a bird with wings and feathers that can act as a *cover* from the stormy blast, from the snares of the devil and from eternal perdition. In this volume, we will focus on the attributes of the eagle.

Romans 1:20

For ever since the creation of the world His invisible attributes, His eternal power and divine nature, have been clearly seen, being understood through His workmanship (all His creation, the wonderful things that He has made), so that they (who fail to believe and trust in Him) are without excuse and without defence.

This scripture tells us that God uses His creations to sometimes teach us about Himself as the Creator and Omnipotent God so that we can appreciate the divine attributes of God.

Hen versus Eagle

According to Webster's dictionary, the eagle is a large bird of prey noted for its strength, size and power of flight. A hen, on the other hand, is described as a female domestic fowl.

Proverbs 23:5 is one of the references in the scriptures that tell us about the eagle. It says, *"Wilt thou set thine eyes upon that which is not? For riches certainly make themselves wings; they fly away as an eagle toward heaven."*

This scripture tells us that the eagle flies toward heaven. The major difference between a hen and an eagle, therefore, is that one is earth-bound while the other is heaven-bound. An eagle flies very high, towards heaven, whilst the hen is earthbound. This difference is important to note as we begin to examine the attributes of the eagle, as shown to us in the scriptures. As we embark on this journey of divine revelation, the Holy Spirit will lead us into a higher level of glory, blessing, favor, and fellowship with God, to the praise of His name.

Introduction

As the eagle belongs in a league of its own, so also is it possible for you to stand out of the pack and be outstanding if you belong to Jesus' league.

Chapter One

The Eagle Flies Toward Heaven Above

In the beginning, God created the Heavens and the earth.

Though we live on the earth, mankind believes there is a Heaven. And, for Christians, we know God's throne is in Heaven, and one day we shall all go to Him. Indeed, Philippians 3:20 says, very clearly, that our citizenship is in heaven, and we eagerly await our Savior from there, the Lord Jesus Christ. That's why Jesus told the thief on the cross, that, *"Today you will be with Me in paradise,"* (Luke 23:43). The scriptures specifically refer to the existence of Heaven.

Matthew 5:34 & 35

> *But I say unto you, Swear not at all; neither by heaven; for it is God's throne: Nor by the earth; for it is his footstool: neither by Jerusalem; for it is the city of the great King.*

Acts 17:24

> *God that made the world and all things therein, seeing that he is Lord of heaven and earth, dwelleth not in temples made with hands.*

Psalms 11:4

> *The Lord is in His holy temple, the Lord's throne is in heaven: His eyes behold, His eyelids try, the children of men.*

Our Lord Jesus Christ taught us to pray in Matthew 6:9: *"our Father, who art in Heaven..."*

In John 8:23, Jesus told the Pharisees, *"Ye are from beneath; I am from **above**: ye are of this world; I am not of this world."* The emphasis is on *heaven* and *above* as opposed to *beneath* or *earth*.

Jesus also said in John 19:11, *"Thou couldest have no power at all against me, except it were given thee from **above**."*

The believer is seated with Christ in Heavenly places, far above principalities and powers (Eph. 2:6, Eph. 1:20). So, you are warring and ruling as kings and priests from a comfortable seated position where, *"you have power to tread on serpents and scorpions, and over all the powers of the enemy: and nothing shall by any means hurt you"* (Luke 10:19).

James 1:17 says, *"Every good gift and every perfect gift is from above, and cometh down from the Father of lights, with whom is no variableness, neither shadow of turning."* We know for sure that heaven is the throne of God, whilst the earth is His footstool (Isa. 66:1 and Acts 7:49). The use of the words "heaven" and "above" clearly show an aspect of God's nature depicted in an eagle. Consequently, since God dwells in the heavens and He owns everything, as His children and citizens of heaven, we must be entitled to some of the blessings from heaven above. By implication, every good and perfect gift is from above and we as believers can lay claim to them.

Gifts That Come from Above

1. The Gift of Grace and Favor

God is the God of all grace and He dispenses it from above.

1 Peter 5:10: *"But the God of all grace, who hath called us unto His eternal glory by Christ Jesus, after that ye have suffered a while, make you perfect, stablish, strengthen, settle you."*

Psalm 30:5: *"For His anger endureth but a moment; in His favour is life…"*

Psalm 84:11: *"For the Lord God is a sun and shield; the Lord bestows grace and favor and honor; no good thing will He withhold from those who walk uprightly."*

Psalm 5:12: *"Thou, Lord, wilt bless the righteous; with favour wilt thou compass him as with a shield."*

2. The Gift of Long Life

The grace to live a long life comes from above. What is the essence of having everything if you don't live long enough to enjoy the fruit of your labor? God promises to satisfy His children with a long life. He says, in Psalm 91:16, *"With long life will I satisfy him, and shew him my salvation."*

Isaiah 65:22 says, *"They shall not build, and another inhabit; they shall not plant, and another eat: for as the days of a tree are the days of my people, and mine elect shall long enjoy the work of their hands."*

Job 5:26 (AMP) says, *"Thou shalt come to thy grave in a full age, like as a shock of corn cometh in his season."*

The psalmist prayed to God in Psalm 71:18 (AMPV), saying, *"Yes, even when I am old and gray-headed, O God, forsake me not, (but kept me alive) until I have declared Your mighty strength to (this) generation, and Your might and power to all that are to come."*

God also promised us, in Isaiah 46:4, *"Even to your old age I am He, and even to hair white with age will I carry you. I have made, and I will bear; yes, I will carry and will save you."*

3. The Gift of Joy

The joy of the Lord is our strength, according to Nehemiah 8:10.

Psalm 103:5 says, *"He will satisfy thy mouth with good things; so that thy youth is renewed like the eagle's."* This is what they call *"ajidewe"* in Yoruba language (Nigeria, West Africa). It means God will satisfy your mouth with good things, which makes you radiate and shine.

4. The Gift of Peace

One of the things God can satisfy you with is peace. If you have all the money in the world and you have no peace, you will be unhappy and will not enjoy the overflowing life that Christ promised us in John 10:10. That is why Jesus Christ said, *"Peace I leave with you, My peace I give unto you: not as the world giveth, give I unto you. Let not your heart be troubled, neither let it be afraid,"* (John 14:27). We all need the peace of God which passes all understanding (Phil. 4:7). To show how important peace is, the Bible says, in Proverbs 25:24 (AMP), *"It is better to dwell in the corner of the housetop than to share a house with a disagreeing, quarrelsome, and scolding woman."* Proverbs 21:19 also says it is better to dwell in the wilderness than with a contentious and angry woman. The opposite of peace is war, trouble, storm, etc. Storms can come in various ways, such as unemployment, unanswered prayers, sickness, grief etc., but, when you have peace, you are made whole.

5. The Gift of Salvation

"For by grace are ye saved through faith; and that not of yourselves: it is the gift of God" (Eph. 2:8). Jesus Christ says in John 6:44 (AMP) that

no man can come to Him, except the Father attracts and draws him and gives him the desire to come to Him. Our good works cannot, on their own, save us, because Isaiah 64:6 reminds us that before God, and without Christ, we are unclean and all our righteousness is as filthy rags. We are only saved by Grace.

6. *The Gift of Prosperity*

Psalm 118:25 says, *"Save now, I beseech Thee, O Lord: O Lord, I beseech Thee, send now prosperity."* The Bible says, in 2 Corinthians 8:9, that Jesus became poor so that we, through His poverty, can be rich. It is God's desire that we prosper; this He expressed through Apostle John in 3 John 1:2, which says, *"Beloved, I wish above all things that thou mayest prosper and be in health, even as thy soul prospereth."* He also takes pleasure in the prosperity of His servants (Ps. 35:27).

Proverbs 18:22 suggested that a good wife is a gift from God. Other categories of good gifts are power, children, wisdom, and the Holy Spirit.

7. *Higher Ground*

When you talk about gifts from above, there are higher levels of things that you should aspire to, that are greater than money. Colossians 3:2 says, *"Set your affection on things above, not on things on the earth."* The eagle-level gift is to give priority to spiritual things above all physical desires.

Matthew 6:31-33, says, *"Therefore take no thought, saying, what shall we eat? or, what shall we drink? or, Wherewithal shall we be clothed? (For after all these things do the Gentiles seek:) for your heavenly Father knoweth that ye have need of all these things. But seek ye first the kingdom of God, and his righteousness; and all these things shall be added unto you."*

Remember that you were saved to serve God (Luke 1:74), and as you serve Him and give priority to the heavenly agenda, God will take care of you and grant you your heart's desire on a platter of gold. The

Bible says, in Job 36:11, *"If they obey and serve Him, they shall spend their days in prosperity, and their years in pleasures."*

A heavenly minded believer will:

- Be interested and committed to the things of the kingdom of heaven.
- Heap up treasures in heaven.
- Reap the fruits of the Spirit: love, joy, peace, patience, etc. (Gal. 5:22-23).
- Be passionate about winning souls for God's kingdom, because this is important to God. The Bible says he who wins souls is wise. The last mandate given to us by Jesus Christ is in Matthew 28: 19-10, which says, *"Go ye therefore, and teach all nations, baptizing them in the name of the Father, and of the Son, and of the Holy Ghost: Teaching them to observe all things whatsoever I have commanded you: and, lo, I am with you always, even unto the end of the world. Amen."*

As the eagle distinguishes itself from the hen by being heaven-bound, so also the believer should be heaven focused and set his heart on things from above, and all the attendant good and perfect gifts that come from above will be his.

Chapter Two

The Anatomy of the Eagle

The Eagle's Wings Gives It Stability When It Soars

Eagles are large, powerfully built birds of prey, *with heavy heads and beaks. Like all birds of prey, eagles have very large, hooked* beaks *for ripping flesh from their prey, strong, muscular legs, and powerful* talons. *The beak is typically heavier than that of most other birds of prey. Eagles' eyes are extremely powerful. It is estimated that the* martial eagle, *whose eye is more than twice as long as a human eye, has a* visual acuity *3.0 to 3.6 times that of humans. This acuity enables eagles to spot potential prey from a very long distance. (2) This keen eyesight is primarily attributed to their extremely large pupils which ensure minimal* diffraction *(scattering) of the incoming light.*

Wikipedia

There is a major difference between the wings of a hen and the wings of an eagle. According to statistics, the eagle's wings are about eight feet long. Proverbs 30:19 tells us about *"The way of an eagle in the air..."* It is not earth-bound like the hen. When flying, the eagle's wings flutter for a while then it glides. In addition, eagles can fly up to an altitude of 10,000 feet.

The eagle's wing gives it stability when it *soars*. It is a symbol of stability. Sometimes in life, we go through ups and downs like Joseph, David, and Naomi. But, when God bears you on eagle's wings, you begin to soar and you get to an altitude where everything becomes stable.

Joseph essentially became the Prime Minister of Egypt, after a lot of ups and downs, and he remained in that *Permanent Place of Blessing* until he died (Gen. 49: 22-24 (AMP)). The children of Israel also, after 430 years of bondage, were borne on eagle's wings to their land of promise. They never returned to Egypt, the land of bondage.

When you talk of stability, you need to think of the Rock of Ages, our *Lord* and Master, Jesus Christ—the Rock of Israel who gives strength and stability. For I proclaim the name (and presence) of the *Lord*; ascribe greatness *and* honor to our God! *"The Rock! His work is perfect, For all His ways are just; A God of faithfulness without iniquity (injustice), just and upright is He."* Deut. 32:3-4 (AMP).

Life was tough for Naomi. In Ruth 1:20-21 (AMP), she said to them,

> *"Do not call me Naomi (sweetness); call me Mara (bitter), for the Almighty has caused me great grief and bitterness. I left full (with a husband and two sons), but the Lord has brought me back empty. Why call me Naomi, since the Lord has testified against me and the Almighty has afflicted me?"*

However, by the time she met the Rock of Ages, her name was restored to Naomi and her joy was full. God wiped away all her tears and silenced her mockers.

The eagle is all by itself when it soars at an altitude of 10,000 ft. in the sky, no predators (even the predators of the air, e.g., a hawk) can prey on it. In the same vein, God is called, "Jehovah El-Elyon," which means the "Most High," No one can be compared to Him. He is in a class of His own.

1. Under His Wings Shall We Trust (Ps. 91:4)

If an eagle can go high and can be protected from predators, how much more can the one who calls Himself Jehovah El-Elyon, Jehovah El Roi? He's a God that is Most High and Higher than the highest (Gen. 14:18-20). Eph.1: 20 -21 (AMP) says, "Which He exerted in Christ when *He raised Him from the dead and seated Him at His (own) right hand in the heavenly (places), far above all rule and authority and power and dominion and every name that is named above every title that can be conferred, not only in this age and in this world, but also in the age and the world which are to come."*

The beauty of this can be found in Ephesians 2:6-7 (AMP) which says, *"and He raised us up together with Him and made us sit down together (giving us joint seating with Him) in the Heavenly sphere (by virtue of our being) in Christ Jesus* (the messiah, the anointed one)." He did this that He might clearly demonstrate through the ages to come the immeasurable (limitless, surpassing) riches of His free grace (His unmerited favor) in (His) kindness and goodness of heart toward us in Christ Jesus."

If Christ is seated far above all powers and principalities, and He says you are sitting next to Him, this means you are also seated far above all powers of the enemy—above poverty, sickness, power, and principalities. As the eagle glides above all, so will you glide over all negative circumstances in life, in Jesus's mighty name. You are untouchable, unconquerable, uncrushable, and unstoppable. You cannot fail because you are seated far above with Christ Jesus.

Jesus says, in Luke 10:19, *"Behold, I give unto you power to tread on serpents and scorpions, and over all the power of the enemy: and nothing shall by any means hurt you."*

Deuteronomy 28:13 says you are supposed to be the head and not the tail; *above only* and not beneath. It is God's purpose for you to soar like an eagle and you shall no longer be the tail or be beneath Jesus's Mighty name.

On whose wings are you flying? Hen's or eagle's wings? If you depend on yourself, Satan or the world to fly, then you are not flying on eagle's wings. But, if you are depending absolutely on God, then you are flying on an eagle's wings. Consequently, you know of a surety that you will get to the top—you belong to the Ivy League, the Jesus League.

2. *The Eagle's Eyes Enable It to See Far Ahead*

The positioning of the eagle's eyes is slanted such that it can see from an altitude of 10,000 ft. For instance, the eagle watches over its eggs from an altitude of 10,000 ft. because its eggs are a delicacy for serpents. Immediately, it spots a serpent approaching its eggs, it flies down swiftly to strike it. The eagle's eyes are said to be among the strongest among the animal kingdom. Research shows that an eagle can spot another eagle soaring from fifty miles away. The eagle's eyes are so strong that eagles are the only creatures that can look directly into the sun. There's no hiding for prey under the eyes of an eagle because of its *color vision*.

It is written in the Bible that where *there is* no vision, the people perish (Prov. 29:18). You need to be able to envision the future, don't plan just for tomorrow. You need to have a long-term vision for yourself, a vision of exceeding greatness. Where you are now is not your end; it is just the beginning that is why those that are looking at you and laughing at you will, in a few months' time, change their minds.

The Bible says, in Micah 7 : 8-10:

Do not rejoice over me (amid my tragedies), O my enemy! Though I fall, I will rise; Though I sit in the darkness (of distress), the Lord is a light for me. I will bear the indignation and wrath of the Lord Because I have sinned against Him, Until He pleads my case and executes judgment for me. He will bring me out to the light, And I will behold His (amazing) righteousness and His remarkable deliverance". Then she who is my enemy will see, And oshame will cover her who said to me, "Where is the Lord your God?" My eyes will see her; Now she will be trampled down Like mud in the streets.

We do not see as God sees, He knows the future; that is why when He called Abraham, He gave him a vision of exceeding greatness. Colour vision, with resolution and clarity, are the most prominent features of eagles' eyes, hence, sharp-sighted people are sometimes referred to as "eagle-eyed." Eagles can identify five (5) distinctly-colored squirrels and locate them even if they were hidden.

In Genesis 12: 1-3, God spoke about greatness to a childless man, but in Genesis 15:2-5, Abraham didn't understand and asked God for an heir. He believed in God for a son, but God had a plan for him to be a father of many nations. God took him out and asked him to look at the stars, and told him as far as his eyes can see, that is the picture of his tomorrow. That is the way you need to envision yourself, your business, your career, your children, your future, etc. See more than the physical because you serve a great God. *"Those who do not plan for the future get extinguished."*

Many businesses deteriorate and close because they didn't plan or continue to evolve. When Lot was to choose a land in Genesis 13:10-18, the Bible says he looked at the plains of Jordan, which is just like looking next door, and chose by sight, not knowing that it was the land of Sodom & Gomorrah, which, eventually, was destroyed by God, with Lot saved by a hair's breadth. But God made Abraham look up to a bigger vision.

Elisha had a vision of a greater tomorrow. So, in 2 Kings 2:3, the sons of the prophets were trying to distract him, he told them to hold their peace and he focused on following Elijah because he had seen greatness, and he eventually received a double portion of the anointing. I don't know the plans you have right now for your future, but God wants you to enlarge your vision and prepare for the glorious future ahead. Aim high, don't compromise, and God will take you there, in Jesus's Name. However, you need to prepare and plan. Joseph prepared himself for his meeting with the Pharaoh by shaving his hair, knowing that Egyptians loathed long hair, Blind Bartimaeus also threw away his old garment in preparation for the next level. You need a vision that will guide and lead you towards your goal.

3. The Eyes of the Lord Are in Every Place

The moon is 382,500 miles away from the earth and the human eyes can see it, and you can also see the little tiny grain in your hand. The eyes of the eagle and the eyes of a man that can see about 400,000 miles away cannot be compared to the eyes of God.

Nothing can escape the eyes of God. The eyes of God see darkness as easily as light. Psalm 139:12 (AMP) says, *"Even the darkness is not dark to You and conceals nothing from You, But the night shines as bright as the day; Darkness and light are alike to You."* He sees your thoughts, He sees your heart, He can reveal secrets and He sees the end from the beginning (Ps. 139:6, 12). Proverbs 15:3 says, "The *eyes of the Lord are in every place, beholding the evil and the good."*

The Bible also says, in Deuteronomy 11:12, *"A land which the Lord thy God careth for: the eyes of the Lord thy God are always upon it, from the beginning of the year even unto the end of the year."* The eyes of the Lord will be upon you, your business, family, and this nation, from the beginning of the year until the end of the year, in Jesus's name.

Psalm 34:15 says, *"The eyes of the Lord are upon the righteous, and His ears are open unto their cry,"* This is why it is important for you to surrender your life to Jesus Christ.

Another feature of the eagle's eyes is its ability to *focus*. "As the eagle descends from the sky to attack its prey, the muscles in the eyes continuously adjust the curvature of the eyeballs to maintain sharp focus and accurate perception throughout the approach and attack," (Wikipedia).

Eagles are said to have double vision, yet they are able to focus on one particular thing at a time. It is one thing to have a vision, but it is another thing, entirely, to focus on that vision. Without focus, you become distracted with a lot of important things seeking for your attention.

The Bible says in Philippians 31:5-16 (MSG),

So, let's keep focused on that goal, those of us who want everything God has for us. If any of you have something else in mind, something less than total commitment, God will clear your blurred vision—you'll see it yet! Now that we're on the right track, let's stay on it.

What do you see?

_____

_____

_____

What are you focusing on?

_____

_____

_____

If you are not seeing the big picture of God for your life, then you are definitely not seeing with God's eyes.

_____

_____

_____

_____

Chapter Three

The Eagle Flies In A League Of Its Own

The eagle flies as high as 10,000 feet. There are 9,956 species of birds in the world and the Peregrine Falcons are the fastest-flying birds in the world. The Bearded Vulture flies as high as 24,000 feet, the Bar-Headed Goose flies as high as 29,000 feet, and the Andean Condor, 15,000 feet. Out of the 9,956 species of birds, there are about three or four birds in the same league as the eagle. *At best, when an eagle is flying, it is flying in the company of another eagle and birds that can fly as high as 10,000 feet and above.*

Therefore, the eagle is in its own league. When it flies high, it is only in the company of eagles or other birds that can fly above 10,000 feet. From these illustrations, God is telling us that an eagle keeps company with eagles. It doesn't mingle with pigeons, hens, or scavengers that feast on dead animals. While other birds like the hen cluck and cackle, seemingly making a lot of noise and chatter as they go in search of food; the eagle flies high and makes less noise while waiting for an opportunity to strike its prey.

The Lord is teaching us, through the characteristics of the eagle, that we need to give closer consideration to the company we keep. The eagle, with other eagles, has the same aspirations to fly high, they have the same strength, and are in the same league encouraging one another.

Eagles are different from about 9,956 other birds, like scavengers or the earthbound birds that flutter.

The eagle stands out, and keeps good company; you can't see an eagle hanging out with a hen. God wants you to stand out, and be outstanding. Proverbs 13:20 says, *"He that walketh with wise men shall be wise: but a companion of fools shall be destroyed."* Proverbs 27:17: *"Iron sharpeneth iron..."*

When you keep good company, you become focused, a high achiever, a team player, and distinct from the multitude. 1 Corinthians 15:33 (AMP) says, *"Do not be so deceived and misled! Evil companionships, communion, associations, corrupt and deprave good manners and morals and character."* If you are in the same company with dogs, you will, in no time, be barking and eat what dogs eat. It is just a question of time.

WHO DO YOU HANG OUT WITH?

In life, major sorrows and setbacks have been traced to the company that people keep—their partners. Sometimes the company you keep determines your destiny. Proverbs 16:29 (AMP) says, *"The exceedingly grasping, covetous, and violent man entices his neighbor, leading him in a way that is not good."* You need to sift through your relationships and the company of friends you keep. Are these relationships adding value to you or to your destiny? What you call *influence* is not neutral—it can either be positive or negative.

So, you can have friends who will either have a positive influence on you or a negative influence. The things that you choose to watch, listen to, or read (music, books, etc.) have a way of influencing you. The people that you hang out with, who don't have positive ambitions in life, will slow you down and mess up your life. It is all about influence and company.

In 2 Chronicles 10: 3-14, Solomon's son, King Rehoboam forsook the counsel of the elders and took the counsel of the young men that were his contemporaries. The kingdom was eventually divided because of the negative counsel inspired by the wrong company he associated with.

Abraham's destiny was temporarily put on hold because he was hanging out with Lot. God instructed Abraham to get out of his country, kindred and father's house, and go to the land He would show him, but Abraham took Lot along, and God stopped speaking to Abraham. It was after Abraham had separated from Lot that God started speaking to him again (Gen. 13:14).

If things concerning you are slow and stagnant, or heaven is silent on your matter, it could be because of the type of people you are hanging out with. God has a glorious destiny for you, and, associating with people who are *strangers to your destiny*, can make God hold back. May God separate you from those that are injurious to your progress, dreams, goals, aspirations, and destiny, in Jesus's name.

You need to break away from the company of time and life wasters—they are destroyers of destiny (Is. 54:16); pretenders, failures, robbers in tithes and offering, armed robbers, betrayers, promise breakers, cheats, gossips, addicts, the proud, procrastinators, discouragers, abusers, copy cats, manipulators, sinners, lazy, envious friends, parasites, liars, drunks, and loafers that are satisfied with an average life.

A loafer

Pray away time wasters using the following scriptures: 2 Corinthians 6:17 says, *"Come out from among them, and be ye separate..."*

Nahum 1:1-12-13:

> *Thus says the Lord: Though they be in full strength and likewise many, even so shall the Assyrians be cut down when their evil counselor shall pass away. Though I have afflicted you Jerusalem, I will not cause you to be afflicted for your past sins any more. For now, will I break his yoke from off you and will burst your bonds asunder.*

Isaiah 10:27 says, *"And it shall come to pass in that day, that his burden shall be taken away from off thy shoulder, and his yoke from off thy neck, and the yoke shall be destroyed because of the anointing."*

Chapter Four

The Eagle Is Fearless

PSALM 91:5-6

> *Thou shalt not be afraid, for the terror by night; nor for the arrow that flieth by day; Nor for the pestilence that walketh in darkness; nor for the destruction that wasteth at noonday.*

One of the qualities of those that belong to the Ivy League is that they have some special qualities that have been subjected to rigorous training, to toughen them up. The eagle possesses some of the characteristics—it is fearless. For a better understanding of the characteristics of an eagle being fearless, let us look at the word fear.

At one level, fear is healthy, it *is an emotion induced by a perceived threat.* It is a natural God-given human emotion. It is a basic survival mechanism; it keeps us alive, and protects us from danger. However, there is also such a thing as unhealthy fear. The Greek word commonly used in the New Testament is Phobos—from which we get the word *phobia*. It is *False Evidence Appearing Real.* Fear can be defined as an unpleasant emotion caused by the threat (real or imagined) of danger, pain or harm. It is a dread, fright, panic, or anxiety, and can cause trembling, shaking, and quivering. Fear can be paralyzing. It can make the heart melt or cause you to break out in a cold sweat.

A classic example of someone who was afraid in the Bible was King Belshazzar, recorded in Daniel 5: 5-6, which says:

In the same hour came forth fingers of a man's hand, and wrote over against the candlestick upon the plaister of the wall of the king's palace: and the king saw the part of the hand that wrote. Then the king's countenance was changed, and his thoughts troubled him, so that the joints of his loins were loosed, and his knees smote one against another.

Scientists have discovered about 700 kinds of phobia including the following:

- Phobia of marriage: gamophobia.
- Phobia for heights: acrophobia.
- Phobia of falling asleep: somniphobia.
- Phobia for rain: ombrophobia.
- Phobia for being without mobile phone coverage: nomophobia.
- Phobia for long words: Hippopotomonstrosesquipedaliophobia.
- Phobia for fear: Phobophobia.

They also include things such as, what is now called FOMO, — the fear of missing out, the fear of not being special. Generally, people suffer from the fear of falling in love or rejection, public speaking, the unknown, darkness, Satan, the future, growing old, loneliness, spiders, messing up, or fear of death.

Some Causes of Fear

- *Thoughts of losing a loved one*
- *Thoughts of sickness or death*
- *Thoughts of losing a child*—sometimes parents worry over the safety of their children. That was how Job felt concerning his children when he constantly made sacrifices for them, saying

peradventure they had sinned against God. *But because fear attracts calamity, what he feared most came upon him and he lost all his children in one day* (Job 3:25).
- *A negative report* can bring fear. For example, a negative medical report causes fear, but you should always believe the report of the Lord that overrides and cancels out every evil report.
- *Ignorance* can also cause fear (if you lack knowledge about someone or a situation).

For example, the Bible says we are not ignorant of the devices of the devil (2 Cor. 2:11). Though the devil roars like a lion, the Bible says, in Isaiah 14:16-17, that we will be surprised at the sight of he that terrorized the whole of mankind. Satan is a defeated foe.

Natural Reaction to Fear

People react to fear in different ways—some would run, hide, or scream, while some would become transfixed, dumb, paralyzed, confused, or powerless. In Job 3:25, we can see that fear attracts calamities. If you harbor fear, it can become a reality. That is why it is important that we do not allow the enemy to sow the seeds of fear in our minds; else it will fester and bring us under the control of Satan. The Bible says, *"God has not given us a spirit of fear, but of power and of love and of a sound."*

Source of Fear

The assault of the enemy comes through the eye and ear gates. Fear is sown into our minds by what we hear or see. For example, concerning Nabal, the Bible says, in 1 Samuel 25:37, *"But it came to pass in the morning, when the wine was gone out of Nabal, and his wife had told him these things that his heart died within him, and he became as a stone."* Just hearing the words of Abigail literally killed him. Also, some people die prematurely when they merely read or hear the doctor's medical report.

But, whose report should you believe? Be careful not to allow Satan to sow and cultivate fear into your mind. Fear is one of the most potent weapons of Satan and it opens a doorway to untold satanic attacks. It is said that the most powerful man can be stripped of all his power by fear.

The patriarchs were afraid at some point in their lives. Abraham was afraid and even lied about Sarah (Gen. 12:11-13, and 20:2). Moses ran away from Egypt because he was afraid (Ex. 2:15). King Saul was afraid of David (1 Sam. 18:12).

In the long run, we see that most fears are unfounded. Isaiah 14:16-17 says, *"They that see thee shall narrowly look upon thee, and consider thee, saying, Is this the man that made the earth to tremble, that did shake kingdoms; that made the world as a wilderness and destroyed the cities thereof; that opened not the house of his prisoners?"* By the time we get to Heaven and see Satan in chains, we will be astonished at the size of him, that has been terrorizing the whole of mankind.

How to Counter Fear

The principal way is through the *knowledge of the Word of God*. Knowledge of the truth drives away the fear of the enemy. Two people can hear the same thing, one will be afraid because he or she lacks knowledge; but the other, that has knowledge, will be calm. If you have knowledge of the truth, you will not be afraid. John 8:32 says, *"And ye shall know the truth, and the truth shall make you free."* The truth will set you free from any kind of fear in, Jesus's mighty name.

Goliath, in 1 Samuel 17:11, was shouting for forty days to instill fear in the hearts of the Israelites, and the king was afraid, but David wasn't afraid. Little did they know that a stone was all they needed to take him out; but David knew the truth: that the battle is the Lord's. To show that his victory was assured, he ran towards Goliath, pulled his sling with a stone to kill him, Goliath fell forward and died. If you know the truth, you will conquer.

One of the greatest truths you need to counteract fear is knowing that **God is with you** (Isa. 41:10-16). One of the last words of Jesus is, *"I will be with you till the end of time."* You can stand against anything once you have knowledge that God is with you. The expression *"do not be afraid"* is one of the most frequent commands in the Bible (John 14:27, Josh. 1:9, Isa. 43:1, Deut. 31:6, 1 Chron. 28:20, Isa. 41:10 and 13, Isa. 54:4).

Psalm 46:1-3:

> *God is our refuge and strength, a very present help in trouble. Therefore, will not we fear, though the earth be removed, and though the mountains be carried into the midst of the sea; Though the waters thereof roar and be troubled, though the mountains shake with the swelling thereof.*

For those that are born-again, it is not only that God is with you, He is in you. Everywhere you go you carry the presence of the Holy Spirit. You need the consciousness, that even in trouble, He will deliver you. Even though you walk through the valley of the shadow of death, you shall fear no evil (Ps. 23:4). Where the Spirit of the Lord is, there is liberty (2 Cor. 3:170). If you are filled with the Holy Ghost, you are bold (2 Tim. 1:7). Don't be anxious for anything (Matt. 6:25-34). God is your hiding place (Ps. 32:6-7, 34:4, 27:1-3, and Rom. 8:31:32).

Who to Fear

Whereas the Spirit of God does not produce negative fear, there is a kind of healthy fear—the fear of God. This does not mean being frightened of God. In fact, it means the opposite. It is an understanding of who God is in relation to us. It means respect, reverence, awe, honor, adoration, and worship; and it could even be translated as love for God. It recognizes the power, majesty, and holiness of God almighty. It leads to a healthy respect of God and is the antidote to all other fears and phobias we experience in life. Fear God and you need not fear anything else or anyone else. It is no coincidence that as the fear of God has decreased in our society; all the other fears have increased.

Ecclesiastes 12:13 says, *"Let us hear the conclusion of the whole matter: fear God, and keep His commandments: for this is the whole duty of man."* And to fear God is the beginning of wisdom (Prov. 1:7, Job 28:28, and Ps. 111:10). Though God is love, He is also a consuming fire (Heb. 12: 28-29). That is why Jesus advised in Luke 12:5, *"But I will forewarn you whom ye shall fear: Fear Him, which after He hath killed hath power to cast into hell; yea, I say unto you, Fear Him."* The Bible also says it is a fearful thing to fall into the hands of the Living God (Heb. 10:31). Do not be a fool; fear God because He has the power to save and to condemn. Do not wait for His judgment, give your life to Him now and accept His gift of salvation.

To be fearless means to be courageous, bold, brave, and confident. Eagles are bold with unshaken confidence, totally devoid of fear and anxiety. It never surrenders to the size or strength of its prey. *The eagle always fights to win.*

Nelson Mandela said, "I learned that courage was not the absence of fear, but the triumph over it. The brave man is not he who does not feel afraid, but he who conquers that fear."

Sometimes, there might be a little fear, but you should encourage yourself in the Lord and say *"God hath not given me the spirit of fear; but of power, and of love, and of a sound mind,"* (2 Tim. 1:7).

The Bible also says, in Isaiah 59:19, *"...when the enemy shall come in like a flood, the Spirit of the Lord shall lift up a standard against him."* Remember, you belong to the *Ivy-League*. If you are born-again and spirit-filled, you may look natural, like the next person, but you are super-natural. The Bible says, in John 17:16, that even though we are in this world, we are not of this world.

The Righteous Are as Bold as a Lion

The eagle is fearless because it knows that it is not an ordinary bird and cannot easily be intimidated. As for us, the Bible says, *"Greater is He that is in you, than he that is in the world."* The Bible says, in Colossians 1: 27, *"Christ in you is the hope of glory,"* not of shame or failure. You are more than a conqueror through Jesus Christ (Rom. 8:37).

You belong to the tribe of the Lion of Judah; Proverbs 30:30 says, *"A lion which is strongest among beasts, and turneth not away for any."* So, the eagle sometimes called the king of birds doesn't turn away from any battle. When it fights, it fights to win.

Since the Lion of the tribe of Judah is your God, you must fight to win because, the Bible says, in 2 Corinthians 2:14, *"...God **always** causes us to triumph in Christ."*

In Colossians 2: 14 -15 (AMP), the Bible says:

> *Jesus Christ cancelled and blotted out and wiped away the handwriting of the note bond with its legal decrees and demands which was in force and stood against us hostile to us. This note with its regulations, decrees, and demands, He set aside and cleared completely out of our way by nailing it to His cross. God disarmed the principalities and powers that were ranged against us and made a bold display and public example of them, in triumphing over them in Him and in it the cross.*

That is why Jesus said, "It is finished!"

The battle has been won already, before the fight. You cannot lose, because Jesus has won the victory over life, poverty, sickness, barrenness, failures, delays, joblessness, childlessness, and every evil.

Psalm 27: 1-3 says,

The Lord is my light and my salvation; whom shall I fear? The LORD is the strength of my life; of whom shall I be afraid? When the wicked, even mine enemies and my foes, came upon me to eat up my flesh, they stumbled and fell. Though a host should encamp against me, my heart shall not fear: though war should rise against me, in this will I be confident.

Anything that is coming against you will stumble and fall because you are an eagle and you belong to the Ivy League. God is our refuge and strength, no matter the situation; we shall not be moved because we are rooted in Christ Jesus. (Ps 46:1-5). Jesus Christ also says, in John 10:28-29, that no one can pluck us from His hands—no power of hell or evil can snatch us out of His hands.

What are the things you are afraid of?

_____

_____

_____

_____

_____

The only fear that is permitted is the reverence fear of the Lord that created you, every other fear should not be tolerated. Always remember what the psalmist said in Psalm 27 and declare it over every form of fear.

1. *The Lord is my light and my salvation; whom shall I fear? the Lord is the strength of my life; of whom shall I be afraid?*
2. *When the wicked, even mine enemies and my foes, came upon me to eat up my flesh, they stumbled and fell.*
3. *Though a host should encamp against me, my heart shall not fear: though war should rise against me, in this will I be confident.*
4. *One thing have I desired of the Lord, that will I seek after; that I may dwell in the house of the Lord all the days of my life, to behold the beauty of the Lord, and to inquire in His temple.*

5. For in the time of trouble He shall hide me in His pavilion: in the secret of his tabernacle shall he hide me; he shall set me up upon a rock.
6. And now shall mine head be lifted up above mine enemies round about me: therefore will I offer in His tabernacle sacrifices of joy; I will sing, yea, I will sing praises unto the Lord.
7. Hear, O Lord, when I cry with my voice: have mercy also upon me, and answer me.
8. When thou saidst, Seek ye My face; my heart said unto thee, Thy face, Lord, will I seek.
9. Hide not Thy face far from me; put not Thy servant away in anger: Thou hast been my help; leave me not, neither forsake me, O God of my salvation.
10. When my father and my mother forsake me, then the Lord will take me up.
11. Teach me Thy way, O Lord, and lead me in a plain path, because of mine enemies.
12. Deliver me not over unto the will of mine enemies: for false witnesses are risen up against me, and such as breathe out cruelty.
13. I had fainted, unless I had believed to see the goodness of the Lord in the land of the living.
14. Wait on the Lord: be of good courage, and he shall strengthen thine heart: wait, I say, on the Lord.

Chapter Five
The Eagle Is Strategic

Another characteristic of the eagle we will consider is that the eagle is strategic. The way the eagle attacks and kills its prey is *strategic*. To be strategic means *drawing a plan to achieve a mission*. A *goal* must precede a *strategy* – there is no strategy without a goal. A *goal/dream* is a target, a mark, an intention, an objective, an aim, a purpose, an ambition, or an aspiration that you want to achieve. The eagle always has a target, mark, aim, purpose, ambition, and aspiration before it attacks its prey.

This is true with most predators – they watch and study their prey closely before attacking. When footballers play soccer, their *goal* is to get the ball into the net. However, to achieve that goal they draw up a *strategic plan* and begin to dribble to the left and to the right in order to achieve the desired target.

The strategy of the footballer is the movement, but the goal is to get the ball into the net. You must have a goal, target, an ambition, and aspiration in life; it will drive you towards achieving your purpose.

Ephesians 5: 15 (AMP) says, *"Look carefully then how you walk! Live purposefully and worthily and accurately, not as the unwise and witless, but as wise, sensible, intelligent people."* You must have a plan to achieve your desired future.

Satan also has Strategies

That is why the Bible says, *"Put on God's whole armor the armor of a heavy-armed soldier which God supplies, that you may be able successfully to stand up against all the strategies and the deceits of the devil"* (Eph. 6: 11 (AMP)).

Delilah had a *goal* to bring *Samson down* and the *strategy* was *seduction* and *persistence*. Satan could not have used the strategy of a duel, because Samson had supernatural strength from God. Therefore, he used a more subtle strategy to achieve his goal. Sometimes, Satan uses alcoholic drink (e.g. Lot) to bait people, but the bait is just an invitation to sin and you have the choice to accept it or not.

God Works in Mysterious Ways

God is a God of strategies; He works in mysterious ways, His wonders to perform. He has strategies for different situations.

For example, the battle strategy He gave Joshua to destroy the walls of Jericho was quite different from the one He gave Jehoshaphat. There are other examples in the Bible of men who were strategic in their walk with God.

Biblical Examples of Divine Strategy

Joseph, From Prison to Palace

Joseph dreamt of his greatness but, he had to be strategic. Despite the fact that he was sold into slavery, lived in Potiphar's house as a servant, but still his strategy was to do the right things to please God. Because his goal was to please God, he was focused on his goal and was able to avoid the bait of Potiphar's wife and found favor everywhere he went (Gen. 39–41).

David, From Shepherd Boy to Giant-Killer

David used strategy when he wanted to kill Goliath. He ran towards him and aimed at Goliath's forehead – the only area that was exposed – and killed him (1 Sam. 17). He knew that because of the size and physical strength of Goliath he could not win at hand-to-hand combat, so he employed a long-range weapon that did not require him to move closer to his target–Goliath.

Jethro – Burden Bearer and Administrator

Jethro acted as a very strategic man. Moses was overwhelmed under the weight of the work and Jethro told him to *delegate* to capable assistants.

Jesus – From Lamb Slain to Risen King

The redemption story is very strategic as it involves the hidden wisdom of God which was unknown to the princes of this world. The Bible says, in 1 Corinthians 2:7-9, *"...for had they known it, they would not have crucified the LORD of glory..."* They thought they were killing Jesus, not knowing that He simply allowed them to crucify Him under the weight of the world's sin so that He could descend to hell to disarm all the powers of darkness, wrestling out of the hand of Satan the keys of hell and death in line with the hidden plan of God to redeem us. Everything that the enemy means for bad, God will turn it around for your own good, in Jesus' name (Gen. 50:20).

Ruth – From Obscurity to Riches

Ruth was strategic to get Boaz's attention, who later married her (Ruth 4).

As a Christian, when you are mapping out your strategies, you must plan with God.

James 4: 13-16 (AMP):

> *Come now, you who say, today or tomorrow we will go into such and such a city and spend a year there and carry on our business and make money. Yet you do not know the least thing about what may happen tomorrow. What is the nature of your life? You are really but a wisp of vapour (a puff of smoke, a mist) that is visible for a little while and then disappears into thin air. You ought instead to say, if the LORD is willing, we shall live and we shall do this or that thing. But as it is, you boast falsely in your presumption and your self-conceit. All such boasting is wrong.*

The rich fool in Luke 12:13-21 planned and didn't put God in the equation. 1 Corinthians 3:6 says, *"I have planted, Apollos watered;* **but God gave the increase."** Proverbs 3:5 says, *"Trust in the LORD with all thine heart; and lean not unto thine own understanding."* Jesus stated in John 15:5 that ... *"without Me you can do NOTHING!"*

Chapter Six

THE EAGLE RIDES THE STORM

Other birds migrate and run away from challenges and storms; eagles fly into it and will use the wind of the storm to rise higher in a matter of seconds. They use the current of the storm to glide higher without having to use their own energy. They are able to do this because God has created them uniquely with an ability to lock their wings in a fixed position in the midst of fierce storm winds.

The revelation is that the eagle knows that, inside every storm, there's a hiding place. It is called *the eye of the storm.* When people are running helter-skelter in the face of a challenge, a person that belongs to the Ivy League with the eagle's anointing would face it headlong, knowing that God is the Lord of the storm.

We can see the workings of this revelation in Exodus 33:22 when God put Moses in a cleft of the rock and protectively covered him with His hands to deliver Moses from the devastating repercussions that could follow any mortal man who sees the glory of God with the naked eye.

Another case in point can be seen in Genesis 26:2-3 & 12, when, in spite of everybody else running away from the land of Egypt during the grievous famine, God informed Isaac not to follow the crowd by going down to Egypt and that He would bless him in that same land.

God was telling Isaac that even in the land of famine, God can favor him by creating a Goshen, a hiding place to enable him to receive his blessings. It is instructive that Isaac obeyed God when it did not make sense by sowing in the barren land and received a hundredfold return in the same year.

When You Walk Through the Fire, He is There

The most secure place is where God is, even in the storm. That is why David was so confident when he said: *"though I walk through the valley of the shadow of death, I will fear no evil for Thou art with me."* Irrespective of what you read about the present state of our economy, try and see beyond the present state of the economy by seeing opportunities, not only challenges. God will distinguish you and make your testimony different from others. For thus saith the Lord, *"Ye shall not see wind, neither shall ye see rain; yet that valley shall be filled with water, that ye may drink, both ye, and your cattle, and your beasts"* (II Kings 3:17). When people are saying there is a casting down, you will say there's a lifting up (Is. 43: 2-7 (AMP), Ps. 23).

Remember, Shadrach, Meshach, and Abednego were thrown into a furnace. The flames of the fire consumed the strong men who threw them in but, as they landed in it, the king saw a fourth man (God) with them. Whenever you need the *fourth man* to step into a situation, I pray He will reveal Himself in Jesus' mighty name.

The Bible says in Hebrews 12:2 that we should imitate our Lord and Master Jesus Christ, who chose to see beyond the horrors of the cross to the *joy* that was set before Him. ***This vision of victory*** helped him to endure the fleeting pain and shame of the cross. At the end of it, He reached His goal, and today, He is sitting at the right hand of God, as a first fruit of the saints triumphant.

In the same vein, when Moses and the children of Israel got to the banks of the Red Sea, the Israelites began to murmur because all they could see were mountains to the right and the left, and the host of pharaoh behind them. But God, who sees differently than we can, saw an expressway in the midst of the Red Sea and informed Moses to encourage the children of Israel to go forward because, according to God's divine plan, the Red Sea must part.

Every Red Sea standing in front of you trying to limit your progress and disgrace you must depart in Jesus' mighty name. The Bible says in Isaiah 14:27 (AMPV), *"For the Lord of hosts has purposed, and who can annul it? And His hand is stretched out, and who can turn it back."* The Psalmist also says in Psalms 33:9, *"For He spoke, and it was done; He commanded, and it stood fast."* So shall it be concerning you in Jesus' name.

Moses was confident to step forward into the Red Sea according to the instruction of God because He knew that the *Breaker*, the *Messiah* had gone ahead of them. Micah 2:13 (AMP) says, *"The Breaker the Messiah will go up before them. They will break through, pass in through the gate and go out through it, and their King will pass on before them, the LORD at their head."* You will break through in Jesus' mighty name.

All you need is for Jesus to be the captain of your boat, for surely though there is a storm, your boat will not sink (Matt. 8:23-27). You should be able to look at every storm in the eye and say, "Peace be still."

What storms are you facing right now?

_____

_____

_____

_____

Is Jesus Christ the captain of your life or you are the captain of your own life?

_____

_____

_____

_____

Without Him you cannot conquer any storm. The arm of flesh will fail you, better put your trust in the Most High who will carry you on His wings through the storms of life. Remember the words of this song by Don Moen–"Still"

STILL

Hide me now
Under Your wings
Cover me
Within Your mighty hand
When the oceans rise and thunders roar I will soar with You above the storm Father You are King over the flood
I will be still and know You are God
Find rest my soul
In Christ alone
Know His power
In quietness and trust
When the oceans rise and thunders roar
I will soar with You above the storm Father You are King over the flood
I will be still and know You are God

Chapter Seven

The Eagle Stirreth Up Her Nest

Deuteronomy 32:11-12 says, *"as an eagle **stirreth** up her nest, fluttereth over her young, spreadeth abroad her wings, taketh them, beareth them on her wings..."* Essentially, this scripture shows that the eagle stirs its eaglets in the nest, flutters over them, carries them, and then drops them; it watches them drop, goes under, and caries them back on her wings. To *stir* means to *unsettle*, to *awaken*, to *arouse, disturb, shake, rustle, blend*. It involves *commotion or disorder*. The eagle stirs up its nest to teach the eaglets how to fly, to prepare them for the future, to train them to mature, to educate them, and to push them out of their comfort zone.

All the rustling and shaking of the eagle is for a purpose and reason. It is to prepare them for a better tomorrow and bring them into maturity so that they can survive in their habitat and defend themselves from predators while developing in them the skills needed to catch their prey. When God says, *"I bare you on Eagles' wings and brought you unto Myself."* This means there is a plan, purpose, and expected destination, and God will not abandon you in the process in Jesus' name.

Deuteronomy 6:23 says, *"He brought us out from thence, that He might bring us in, to give us the land which He sware unto our fathers."* He bought them out of Egypt that He might take them to the Promised

Land. The plan of God is to take you out of slavery, poverty, penury, sorrow, calamity, failure to take you to higher ground! He has a plan and He has a purpose, you will not perish, you will reach your goal, the plan of God to take you higher will start from now, in Jesus' name.

The eagle disturbs its children so that it can toughen them; make them alert and more conscious of the environment they live in. When they are in the nest, they are open to predators, but when they begin to fly on their own, they are no longer victims; they become responsible and make decisions on their own. When you are a baby, you drink milk under the control of tutors and governors, but when you mature, you begin to eat strong meat and crack bones, you develop your senses and are able to fulfill your God-given destiny (Gal. 4:1-5, Heb. 5:13-14).

The eagle repeatedly stirs up her young until they reach perfection. The same thing God does with us. Proverbs 22:6 says, *"Train up a child in the way he should go: and when he is old, he will not depart from it."* As the eagle trains and pushes its eaglets, God also trains and pushes His children. We also need to train our children and push them so that we will not have regrets in the future.

We have established that the eagle continuously trains its eaglets until they reach perfection. Training must be continuous. There are some professions that take examinations every year to renew their licenses so that they do not remain on the same level or their skills become irrelevant or obsolete. As the eagle repeatedly trains its eaglets, we need to also undergo continuous training.

As parents, the Bible encourages us to *"Train up a child in the way he should go: and when he is old, he will not depart from it"* (Prov. 22:6). Susannah Wesley believed that for a child to grow into a *self-disciplined* adult, he/she must first be a *parent-disciplined* child. To her, the stubborn flesh was the hardest battle for Christians to fight, and godly parents would do well to equip their children to overcome it early.

She writes:
When the will of a child is totally subdued, and it is brought to revere and stand in awe of the parents, then a great many childish follies may be

passed by. I insist on the conquering of the will of children betimes, because this is the only strong and rational foundation of a religious education when this is thoroughly done, then a child is capable of being governed by reason and piety.

Here are sixteen rules she laid down in her home.

1. Eating between meals is not allowed.
2. As children, they are to be in bed by 8 p.m.
3. They are required to take medicine without complaining.
4. Subdue self-will in a child, and those working together with God to save the child's soul.
5. To teach a child to pray as soon as he can speak.
6. Require all to be still during family worship.
7. Give them nothing that they cry for, and only that when asked for politely.
8. To prevent lying, punish no fault which is first confessed and repented of.
9. Never allow a sinful act to go unpunished.
10. Never punish a child twice for a single offense.
11. Comment and reward good behavior.
12. Any attempt to please, even if poorly performed, should be commended.
13. Preserve property rights, even in the smallest matters.
14. Strictly observe all promises.
15. Require no daughter to work before she can read well.
16. Teach children to fear the rod.

Upgrade Yourself

It is not good for you to stay in one place, you must retool yourself, attend workshops instead of spending all your income on food and clothes, you need to improve and upgrade yourself so that you can remain relevant.

Indeed, Proverbs 18:16 says, *"A man's gift maketh room for him, and bringeth him before great men."* The business people call it branding. Branding means refurbishing yourself. It also means having a unique identity so that you can stand out. Companies rebrand to become more relevant, noticeable and thereby improve their profitability and market share. You need to rebrand yourself.

God Uses the Wilderness as a Training Ground

The stirring up involves pain and discomfort. Sometimes, you do not always understand the reason why God brings a shaking into your life. Psalm 103:7 says, *"He made known His ways unto Moses, His acts unto the children of Israel."* God took the Israelites from a comfortable place in Goshen, Egypt, bore them on Eagles' wings and dropped them in the wilderness for forty years. A wilderness is a jungle, deserted place, uncomfortable place, a place of dryness, naturally a place of want and need.

In the course of the eagle training her young ones to fly, it would appear for a moment that the eagle had abandoned them to their fate, but in the nick of time, before they crash to the ground, it swoops under them and carries them on its back in a most reassuring way. Sometimes, when we are going through a wilderness experience, we might feel lonely, dejected and abandoned by God. But the Bible says, in Deuteronomy 33:22, that underneath us are His everlasting arms to hold us up and save us from imminent dangers. The end of the LORD is always good.

The wilderness is a training ground. 2 Timothy 2:3 says, *"Thou therefore endure hardness, as a good soldier of Jesus Christ."* As the eagle trains and takes care of its eaglets so does God train us, takes care of us and teaches us.

In Deuteronomy 29:5-6, the Bible says God made sure that even though the children of Israel were in the wilderness, their shoes did not wear out, neither did their clothes wax old. When they were thirsty, He gave them water from the rock. When they were hungry, He fed them with manna from heaven. He protected them from fiery serpents and scorpions and thereby sustained His people for forty years. In all of this, God was teaching them to depend solely on Him for their sustenance and not the arm of flesh.

When you are going through a period of dryness, you need to look for the lessons to be learned, as God is always a God of purpose and plan. In Numbers 11: 4-6; 21-23; 31, God showed His children that it was not because He could not feed Six-Hundred-Thousand (600,000) footmen, (not counting women and children) with quail overnight in the middle of nowhere, all He needed was to send a wind.

This shows that God deliberately gave them manna for forty years just to teach them to learn to depend solely on Him for their provision. It is instructive in Scriptures that after God swarmed the camp with heaps of quails, He smote the rebellious ones that did not understand the ways and the teachings of God and started murmuring and lusting after varieties of food they were used to in Egypt, the land of bondage. What a great lesson to learn from their experience.

We need to realize that when we go through trials and tribulations, it is usually just a test. The Bible says in Proverbs 3:12, *"For whom the LORD loveth He correcteth; even as a father the son in whom he delighteth."* God chastises those He loves (Heb. 12:6).

David said in Psalm 119:71 that *"it is good for me that I have been afflicted; that I might learn thy statutes."* Instead of murmuring, just pray to learn the lesson you are supposed to learn. In 1 Kings 17:3-4, He told Elijah to go to the Brook Cherith during a grievous famine for three and a half years, and that He will send ravens to feed him. However, eventually, the brook dried up. God told the prophet to go to the city of Zarephath in Zidon and that He had commanded a poor widow that had a last meal to eat and die, to sustain him for three years.

To a carnal person, this would have been laughable if not impossible – a widow with her last meal? But such are the ways of God. This teaches us not to look down on anyone for our God is a wonder-working God whose ways are past finding out. We serve a God who maketh poor, and maketh rich: He bringeth low, and lifteth up. He raiseth up the poor out of the dust, and lifteth up the beggar from the dunghill, to set them among princes (1 Sam. 2:7-8). The Bible says in 2 Kings 3:17, *"Ye shall not see wind, neither shall ye see rain; yet that valley shall be filled with water, that ye may drink, both ye, and your cattle, and your beasts."*

Sometimes things happen in our lives that we don't understand, but, at the end, God ensures that all things work together for our good.

Joseph went through trials for about seventeen years, but in retrospect, God was hiding him until his appointed time. If Joseph was released from prison before the expiration of two years as he wanted, the best that could have happened to him is that he would have gone back to Potiphar's house to be a servant or found another job.

However, God kept him in prison until there arose a problem in Egypt that only He could solve, which eventually caused Joseph to become the Prime Minister of Egypt.

John the Baptist: God hid him until the time came for him to be showed unto Israel. For a season, John's parents were termed barren but the end justified the means because Jesus says, *"Among those that are born of women there is not a greater prophet than John the Baptist"* (Matt. 11:11).

Hannah, Samuel's mother: It was surely worth the wait. Samuel's mother was barren until the right time when there was a vacuum that needed to be filled in the priesthood.

Instead of complaining, please remember that God is working out His purposes in your life. God has a plan; He is testing and teaching you all through the waiting period. If today you are experiencing a delay, God is saying "***Don't give up!***" The suffering can never be forever, in the midst of your trial God will be with you (Isa. 43:2-3).

Apostle Paul: In II Corinthians 12:7-9, God gave a thorn in the flesh to Paul because God didn't want him to be proud, he prayed three times and God told him he needed the situation in his life and Paul said, *"His grace is sufficient for me."* While you are in the wilderness, His grace will sustain you in Jesus' name. Please note that the suffering or the wilderness experience can only be for a while because the Bible says, in 1

Peter 5: 10, *"but the God of all grace, who hath called us unto His eternal glory by Christ Jesus, after that ye have suffered a while, make you perfect, stablish, strengthen, settle you."*

For the children of Israel, this nature of God proved true in that a time came when they reached the Promised Land, **behold** the manna they have been eating for forty years ceased and they began to eat the fruits of the land (Joshua 5:12). I prophesy into your life that a big change is coming over you now that the lessons have been learnt, the waiting is over, the manna has ceased and it is time for you to enter into your wealthy place and begin to eat the good of our land, and even beyond.

Isaiah 1:19 says, *"If ye be willing and obedient, ye shall eat the good of the land."*

It is not all those that left Egypt that made it to the Promised Land; a lot of people died because of unbelief and sin. If you are a sinner, you are not guaranteed that your tomorrow will be alright. Isaiah 3:10-11 says, *"Say to the righteous that it shall be well with them, for they shall eat the fruit of their deeds. Woe to the wicked! It shall be ill with them, for what their hands have done shall be done to them.*

Chapter Eight
The Rebirth Of An Eagle

An eagle has the longest life-span of its species. It can live up to seventy years, but to reach this age, the eagle must make some tough decisions. In its fortieth year, its long, flexible talons can no longer grab prey for food. Its long and sharp beak begins to bend. In old age, its heavy wings, due to their thickness, sticks to its chest, making it difficult to fly.

Then, the eagle is left with only two options: die or go through the painful process of change. The change process requires that the eagle fly to a mountain top and sit on its nest. There, it knocks its beak against a rock until it plucks it out, then the eagle waits for a new beak to grow before it plucks out the talons. When the new talons grow back, the eagle starts plucking its thick, heavy feathers. After this, the eagle takes its famous flight of rebirth and lives for another thirty years. Why is the change needed? To survive and live.

1.1 He Shall Renew Your Youth

The Bible describes this rebirth in Psalm 103:4, which says, *"Who satisfieth thy mouth with good things; so that thy youth is renewed like the eagles."* The change process for the eagle involves a lot of pain. If you are dieting and exercising, you have to sustain it, and at the end of the day, you will look greater than when you started.

Dieting and exercises are okay, but there is an ultimate to staying fit which is a grace that comes from God. Isaiah 40:2831 (AMP) says, *"....But those who wait for the LORD (who expect, look for, and hope in Him) shall change and renew their strength and power; they shall lift their wings and mount up close to God as eagles mount up to the sun; they shall run and not be weary, they shall walk and not faint or become tired."* This is supernatural.

Naturally, as you grow old, your strength should wane and abate, but God gives you the grace such that when young people are tired, your strength is renewed. If you are born again, you are supernatural; you are a visitor on this earth, and heaven is your home. Your resources are supplied from heaven (Phil. 4:19). God can give you extraordinary strength, and bless you beyond the usual so that when people are complaining, you would have nothing to complain about. There is nothing wrong with doing the physical exercises and dieting, but there is something extra that you can get from God.

Caleb said in Joshua 14:10-12 (AMP), *"And now, behold, the LORD has kept me alive, as He said, these forty-five years since the LORD spoke this word to Moses, while the Israelites wandered in the wilderness; and now, behold, I am this day eighty-five years old. Yet I am as strong today as I was the day Moses sent me; as my strength was then, so is my strength now for war and to go out and to come in..."*

It is possible to feel forty years old at eighty years old. This is a grace from God. Deuteronomy 34:7 says, *"Moses was one hundred and twenty years old when he died: his eye was not dim, nor his natural force abated."* This means Moses could still father a child even at old age. Abraham's and Sarah's bodies were dead, but they believed, waited on the promise of God for a child, and it was counted unto them for righteousness (Rom. 4:17-24 (AMP), Gen. 17:17, Gen. 18:12, Gen. 21:7).

There is nothing that you are believing God for in this season that will be denied you, in Jesus' name because God can override natural forces. Psalm 92:14 says, *"They shall still bring forth fruit in old age; they shall be fat and flourishing."* You will be lively and vigorous even in old age in Jesus' name (Psalm 91:16).

God promises us in John 10:10 (AMP) that *"...I came that they may have and enjoy life, and have it in abundance to the full, till it overflows."* Normally, as you grow old, your strength should wane, but as you grow old, your strength would continue to wax stronger which is not natural, it is a grace (Deut. 33:25b). Hezekiah was sick and close to death when he looked to God and said, *"Remember now, O LORD, I pray, how I have walked before You in truth,"* and God added fifteen more years to his life (2 Kings 20:3). If you feel weak, I pray that God will exchange your weakness for His strength in Jesus' name (Joel 3:10).

When Paul had his problems, 2 Corinthians 12:9-10 says God told him, *"My grace is sufficient for you."* The grace you need to excel in life, to be above only and not beneath, God will grant it to you today, in Jesus' name. When you are weak, God exchanges that weakness for the life of God (2 Cor. 4:712). You will live life to the fullest. Psalm 118:17 says, *"I shall not die but live, and declare the works of the LORD."*

The eagle breaks off its beak so that a new one can grow. The scripture that aligns with this change can be found in 2 Corinthians 5:17, which says, *"Therefore if any man be in Christ, he is a new creature: OLD THINGS ARE PASSED AWAY; BEHOLD, ALL THINGS ARE BECOME NEW."*

Examples of Old Things That Must Pass Away

Bad Habits: E.g., character change such as heavy partying, smoking, not paying your tithes, a prayerless life, laziness, bad temper, gossiping, unforgiveness, worrying, procrastination, lying, low self-esteem, etc.

1 Corinthians 6: 9-11 (AMP):

Do you not know that the unrighteous will not inherit or have any share in the kingdom of God? Do not be deceived; neither the sexually immoral, nor idolaters, nor adulterers, nor effeminate (by perversion), nor those who participate in homosexuality, nor thieves, nor the greedy, nor drunkards, nor revilers (whose words are used as weapons to abuse, insult, humiliate, intimidate, or slander), nor swindlers will inherit or have any share in the kingdom of God. And such were some of you (before you believed). But you were washed (by the atoning sacrifice of Christ), you were sanctified (set apart for God, and made holy), you were justified (declared free of guilt) in the name of the Lord Jesus Christ and in the (Holy) Spirit of our God (the source of the believer's new life and changed behavior).

Colossians 3:8 (AMP) – *"But now rid yourselves (completely) of all these things: anger, rage, malice, slander and obscene (abusive, filthy, vulgar) language from your mouth."*

1. Doubt, Unbelief, and Fear: 1 Timothy 1:7 says, *"For God hath not given us the spirit of fear; but of power, and of love, and of a sound mind."*
2. Poverty: 2 Corinthians 8:9 says, *"For ye know the grace of our LORD Jesus Christ, that, though He was rich, yet for your sakes He became poor, that ye through His poverty might be rich."*
3. Sorrow: Psalm 30:5 says, *"…weeping may endure for a night, but joy cometh in the morning."*
4. Sickness: James 5:15, *"And the prayer of faith shall save the sick, and the Lord shall raise him up. And if he has committed sins, they shall be forgiven him."* AMP 1 Peter 2 Vs 247.
5. Limitation, Stagnancy and Lack. Philippians 4:19–*And my God will liberally supply (fill until full) your every need according to His riches in glory in Christ Jesus.*

Things That Must Become New *(Rev. 21:5, Ps. 126:1-4)*

The only thing that does not die and remains constant can be seen in Matthew 24:35, which says, *"Heaven and earth shall pass away, but my words shall not pass away."* And in Mathew 5:18, which says, *"For verily I say unto you, till heaven and earth pass, one jot or one tittle shall in no wise pass from the law, till all be fulfilled."*

1. Your Heart. Psalm 51:10-12 – "*Create in me a clean heart, O God, And renew a right and steadfast spirit within me. Do not cast me away from Your presence. And do not take Your Holy Spirit from me. Restore to me the joy of Your salvation And sustain me with a willing spirit" (Ps. 139:23-24* (AMP)).
2. Your relationship with God must be renewed. Romans 5: 1- 2: "*Therefore, since we have been justified (that is, acquitted of sin, declared blameless before God) by faith, (let us grasp the fact that) we have peace with God (and the joy of reconciliation with Him) through our Lord Jesus Christ (the Messiah, the Anointed) Through Him we also have access by faith into this (remarkable state of) grace in which we (firmly and safely and securely) stand. Let us rejoice in our hope and the confident assurance of (experiencing and enjoying) the glory of (our great) God (the manifestation of His excellence and power).*"
3. Your mind must be renewed. Ephesians 4:24-25
Romans 12:2: "*And do not be conformed to this world (any longer with its superficial values and customs), but be transformed and pro*-gressively changed (as you mature spiritually) by the renewing of your mind (focusing on godly values and ethical attitudes), so that you *may prove (for yourselves) what the will of God is, that which is good and acceptable and perfect (in His plan and purpose for you).*"
4. The new man must emerge. Colossians 3:9-10: *Do not lie to one another, for you have stripped off the old self with its evil* practices, and have put on the new (spiritual) self who is being continually renewed in true knowledge in the image of Him who created the new self."

1.2 God's Eternal Purpose is to Reconcile Man to Himself

God says in Exodus 19:4, "*Ye have seen what I did unto the Egyptians, and how I bare you on eagles' wings, and brought you unto Myself.*" What did

He do to the Egyptians? The ten plagues God brought on the Egyptians was a divine demonstration of God's determination to deliver the Israelites to enable them serve Him. After crossing the Red Sea, the children of Israel looked backed and Moses said *"The Egyptians whom ye have seen today, ye shall see them again no more forever, and it was so"* (Ex. 14:13).

The same God that brought upon the Egyptians the ten plagues will destroy all your adversaries and enemies in Jesus' name. Our deliverance comes because we need to serve God as it is written in Luke 1:74, *"That he would grant unto us, that we being delivered out of the hand of our enemies might serve him without fear."* God brought the Israelites unto Himself so that they may serve Him. Today, as you are delivered from poverty, sickness, barrenness, depression, lack, failure and untimely death, it is so that you can serve God.

God is using the deliverance to bring you to Himself (Ps. 118:17). His plan is to take you out of bondage into your wealthy place, not waste your life in the wilderness like the children of Israel who were doing a funeral march to nowhere. *"And He brought us out from thence, that He might bring us in, to give us the land which He sware unto our fathers"* (Deut. 6:23).

As Joseph was delivered from the jail, he stepped out to become the Prime Minister because God had a plan and purpose for him. As God delivers you from your bondage, you will step on higher grounds, in Jesus' mighty name.

Jesus says in John 3:7, *"Marvel not that I said unto thee, ye must be born again."* Your old life must pass away and you must be born-again because there is a new covenant in the Blood of Jesus that He shed for us (Luke 22: 20)

God wants to do something new in your life this season. Your old life and the things that cause you pain can be taken away, and God will give you a new lease of life. Drop your old life and surrender your life to Jesus Christ. As an eagle, you belong to the (in-crowd) Ivy league, and it is time to quit being influenced negatively by scavengers and those that have no vision, no hope, and aliens from the commonwealth of Israel.

1.3 THE JESUS' LEAGUE: THE IN-CROWD

In every organization, institution or association, there's usually a select cluster of people that have privileged information, are exposed to opportunities, benefits, and advantages that the larger group of people do not have access to. They are separate, special, set apart from the multitude, they stand out – these are the people called the "in-crowd."

Then there is the other set of people; the larger group, the multitude, whom we can call "the out-crowd." In life, people will do virtually everything to belong to the in-crowd; they struggle to be accepted and sometimes compromise standards just to be accepted. Those that do not belong to the in-crowd feel rejected, downcast, ostracized and maybe hurt.

Nonetheless, for us as Christians, even though we are in this world, we are not of this world (John 17:16). Quit struggling so hard to belong or conform to this world; you're fearfully and wonderfully made. You are a brand (Zech. 3:2), so, instead of struggling to be part of them, they are supposed to seek you out. It doesn't matter if the world rejects you, as long as God accepts you; you are on the right track.

When Jesus was on earth, He created His own elite club—the in-crowd of Jesus Christ. The members of the in-crowd of Jesus are called disciples. A disciple is a disciplined follower of Christ. In Matthew 28:19, Jesus said, *"Make disciples of all nations."* The disciples had privileges (Matthew 13:1-3,11-17; Matthew 5). Everything written in Matthew 5 and 6 was for the disciples, not the multitude. If you belong to Jesus' in-crowd, there is peace, riches, protection, and eternal life (Phil. 4:19).

Choices

However, there is an entry requirement to be in Jesus' League. You may ask "How then do I belong to this in-crowd? Jesus says, "come as you are" – it is a general invitation to everyone. He will not reject you, but you must come to Him. There is no other way outside Jesus; unlike the world's system, it is not dependent on who you know or how much you have. Jesus is the way, the truth and the life, no one can be enrolled into this league except through Jesus Christ. Nonetheless, you have to make a choice, Jesus is not going to force Himself on you, He allows everybody to use their free will. Life, as we all know is full of choices.

Matthew 7:13-15 says: *"You can enter God's kingdom only through the narrow gate. The highway to hell is broad, and its gate is wide for the many who choose that way. But the gateway to life is very narrow and the road is difficult, and only a few ever find it."*

Every blessed day that we wake up, we are confronted with choices and whatever we choose to do or not do has a way of determining our tomorrow. For example, when we woke up this morning, we had a choice to say a prayer or not. Some of us just woke up and went on with the chores and the things we wanted to do for the day. The way we see you is a product of your choice that you have made, the things that you have considered. Whether you read your Bible as you wake up in the morning, what you had for breakfast or what clothes you wear. Your decisions, choices you make are informed by the things you do and my prayer is that God will help us to make good choices in Jesus' name.

Jesus is setting before us choices, and usually, in life, there are two ways, or two choices–right or wrong, good or bad, life or death, heaven or hell, righteousness or unrighteousness. There is no middle ground–it is either you belong to Jesus or you belong to Satan; it is either God is your father or Satan is your father. Jesus says in Revelation 3: 15 & 16 that, *"I know thy works, that thou art neither cold nor hot: I would thou wert cold or hot. So then because thou art lukewarm, and neither cold nor hot, I will spue thee out of my mouth."* Jesus presents to us two ways – the broad and narrow ways.

In the broad way, life is easy with a lot of liberties: drinking, smoking, lying, wild partying, stealing, sexual immorality, unforgiveness, gambling, indecent dressing, hatred, etc. If you are on the broadway, you live your life the way you want to, nobody will force you to read your Bible or pray; you are your own god, with nobody to tell you what is right or wrong. You live as you like, you are the boss, no one will question your decisions or actions. It seems pleasurable and attractive but the Bible gave a warning in Proverbs 14:12 that:

- *There is a way which seemeth right unto a man, but the end thereof are the ways of death.* (KJV)
- *There is a path before each person that seems right, but it ends in death.* (NLT)
- *There is a way which seems right to a man and appears straight before him, but at the end of it is the way of death.* (AMP)

It was said of Moses, in Hebrews 11:25, that he chose to suffer affliction with the people of God than to enjoy the fleeting pleasures of sin.

Conversely, narrow is the way which leads unto life and few there be that find it." Why did the Bible say, *narrow is the way*? Here, there are rules, regulations, constraints, there is a price to pay; sacrifices, self-control/discipline, prayers, fasting, commitment, ... that is why the road is narrow. Unlike the broad way, there are no excuses on the narrow road.

What are the pressures on the narrow road?

_____

_____

_____

_____

_____

"*The few that make it belong to the Jesus League*".

Self-denial

Jesus said, in Matthew 5:44:

But I say unto you, **Love your enemies, bless them that curse you, do good to them that hate you,** *and* **pray for them which despitefully use you, and persecute you;** *That ye may be the children of your Father which is in heaven: for he maketh his sun to rise on the evil and on the good, and sendeth rain on the just and on the unjust. For if ye love them which love you, what reward have ye? do not even the publicans the same? And if ye salute your brethren only, what do ye more than others? do not even the publicans so? Be ye therefore perfect, even as your Father which is in heaven is perfect.*

Luke 9:23 says, *"if any man comes after me, let him deny himself and take up his cross daily and follow me."*

A cross is an unattractive symbol of suffering, it's hard. In Luke 14:25-27, it says,

And there went great multitudes with him: and he turned, and said unto them. If any man come to me, and hate not his father, and mother, and wife, and children, and brethren, and sisters, yea, and his own life also, he cannot be my disciple. And whosoever doth not bear his cross, and come after me, cannot be my disciple.

In II Timothy 2:3-5, the Bible says:

"Thou therefore endure hardness, as a good soldier of Jesus Christ. No man that warreth entangleth himself with the affairs of this life; that he may please him who hath chosen him to be a soldier. And if a man also strive for masteries, yet is he not crowned, except he strive lawfully."

1 Corinthian 9:24-27 (AMP)

Do you not know that in a race all the runners compete, but (only) one receives the prize? So run (your race) that you may lay hold (of the prize) and make it yours. Now every athlete who goes into training conducts himself temperately and restricts himself in all things. They do it to win a wreath that will soon wither, but we (do it to receive a crown of eternal blessedness) that cannot wither. Therefore I do not run uncertainly (without definite aim). I do not box like one beating the air and striking without an adversary. But (like a boxer) I buffet my body (handle it roughly, discipline it by hardships) and subdue it, for fear that after proclaiming to others the Gospel and things pertaining to it, I myself should become unfit (not stand the test, be unapproved and rejected as a counterfeit).

On the narrow road, you cannot carry baggage, no excess load, you need to drop unforgiveness and every sin. Hebrews 12:1 says, "*Wherefore seeing we also are compassed about with so great a cloud of witnesses, let **us lay aside every weight**, and the sin which doth so easily beset us, and let us run with patience the race that is set before us.*"

Because it is very narrow, there are temptations and suffering sometimes. Why must I give my first fruit; why must I pay tithe; why can't I just spend all the hundred percent? That's pressure. In the narrow road, you may bend sometimes, you may trip sometimes; but we thank God that, in Matthew 11:29-30, Jesus Christ says, "*take My yoke up on you and learn of Me for I am gentle and meek and humble in heart, you will find rest.*" My yoke is not that difficult, the Holy Spirit will help you. "*My yoke is wholesome, useful, good, not hash, not pressing but gracious, comfortable and pleasant and my burden is light.*"

That's why in Philippians 3:7-7, "*Paul says that everything I have, I count it as nothing.*" He says the most important thing for me to win

Christ, to make heaven, to find that road that leads to life–that is my main focus in life.

Jesus Christ tells us in John 14:6, *"I am the way, the truth and the life, no man cometh to the Father but by Me."* He says, *"I am the way that you have been looking for."*

John 10:9,10: *"I am the door: by Me if any man enter in, he shall be saved, and shall go in and out, and find pasture. The thief cometh not, but for to steal, and to kill, and to destroy: I am come that they might have life, and that they might have it more abundantly."*

Acts 4:12: *"Neither is there salvation in any other: for there is none other name under heaven given among men, whereby we must be saved."*

1 John 5:12, says, *"He that has the Son has life, He that has not the Son has not life."* It is so clear. If Jesus Christ is not your personal Lord and Savior, you don't have life, you can't find the way, you cannot make it.

John 3:5 says, *"Except you are born again, you cannot enter, you can't see and you cannot enter, God is not mocked."*

II Timothy 2:19 says, *"don't be fooled, the foundation of God standeth sure; God knows those that are His own, He knows those that are on the narrow way, those that endure, those that will do anything to make it, those that are under His rule that are obedient, that are doing what is right."* Many may think or assume that they are on the narrow way but may not, only God knows. By their fruits He says, you shall know them. Scriptures have said that many are called but few are chosen, and they are called the Jesus League.

You have a choice–the broad way with all the liberties and the narrow way with all the constraints.

If you are willing to repent and surrender your life to Jesus Christ, then pray this prayer right now:

1.4 Prayer of Salvation

LORD Jesus, I come to You,
I know I am a sinner,

Please forgive me of my sins.
With my mouth, I confess that Jesus Christ is the LORD of my life;
With my heart, I believe that it is because of me that You came into this world.
You died and took away all my sins. Take away my burdens also,
Write my name in the Book of Life,
Fill me with Your Holy Spirit,
And make my old life pass away
Enlist me into Your in-crowd in Jesus' name. Amen.

References

https://archive.org/stream/royalnaturalhist47lyde/royalnaturalhist-47lyde#page/n241/mode/1up,

Don Moen Lyrics "Still" AZlyrics.com

John Wesley's Mom

Raising Godly Children, March 29, 2011

16 House Rules by Susannah Wesley

Lightning Source UK Ltd.
Milton Keynes UK
UKHW021053050520
362811UK00013B/683